STAGE 1

HOW TO BE A
Nature Detective

by Millicent E. Selsam

illustrated by Marlene Hill Donnelly

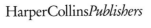

HarperCollinsPublishers

The *Let's-Read-and-Find-Out Science* book series was originated by Dr. Franklyn M. Branley, Astronomer Emeritus and former Chairman of the American Museum–Hayden Planetarium, and was formerly co-edited by him and Dr. Roma Gans, Professor Emeritus of Childhood Education, Teachers College, Columbia University. Text and illustrations for each of the books in the series are checked for accuracy by an expert in the relevant field. For a complete catalog of Let's-Read-and-Find-Out Science books, write to HarperCollins Children's Books, 10 East 53rd Street, New York, NY 10022.

Let's Read-and-Find-Out Science is a registered trademark of HarperCollins Publishers.

The illustrations in this book were painted in watercolor and pen and ink on Arches cold press paper.

The text was first published in a different form under the title *Nature Detective*.
Harper & Row, Publishers published *How to Be a Nature Detective* in 1966.

How to Be a Nature Detective

Library of Congress Cataloging-in-Publication Data
Selsam, Millicent Ellis, date.
   How to be a nature detective / by Millicent E. Selsam ; illustrated by Marlene Hill Donnelly.
      p.   cm. — (Let's-read-and-find-out science. Stage 1)
   Summary: Anyone can learn to be a nature detective and tell what animals have been around, if he learns to recognize the clues, especially different footprints.
   ISBN 0-06-023447-4. — ISBN 0-06-023448-2 (lib. bdg.)
   ISBN 0-06-445134-8 (pbk.)
   1. Animal tracks—Identification—Juvenile literature.   2.   Tracking and trailing—Juvenile literature.   [1. Animal tracks.   2.   Tracking and trailing.] I. Donnelly, Marlene Hill, ill.   II. Title.   III. Series.
QL768.S44   1995   93-28523
599'.05—dc20   CIP
                                                                          AC

Typography by Christine Kettner
10 9 8 7 6 5 4 3 2 1
❖
Revised and Newly Illustrated Edition

HOW TO BE A
Nature Detective

"What happened?" a detective says.

"Who was here?

"Where did he go?"

A detective has many ways to find out.

One way is to look for the marks someone or something has made—fingerprints, footprints, the tracks made by bike tires.

Sometimes a detective finds a hair, a button, a piece of torn clothing. All these things are clues. They help a detective answer these questions: What happened? Who was here? Where did he go?

You can be a detective too, a special kind of detective—
a nature detective.

Nature detectives find tracks and clues that answer
these questions: What animal walked here? Where did it go?
What did it do? What did it eat?

Where does a nature detective look for clues?
Almost anywhere—in a backyard, in the woods, in a city park.
You can find tracks in many places—in mud, in snow,
in sand, in dust, even on the sidewalk or on the floor.
Wet feet or wet muddy paws can make tracks anywhere.

Here is a problem for a nature detective:

Here is a cat.

Here is a dog.

Here is a dish for the cat. 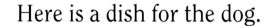Here is a dish for the dog.

The cat's dish had milk in it. The dog's dish had meat in it.

Who drank the milk? Who ate the meat?

Look at the tracks and see.

Look at the tracks that go to the cat's dish. They were made by an animal that walks on four feet. And you can see claw marks in front of the toe marks.

A cat has four feet and sharp claws. But so does a dog. Who went to the cat's dish?

We still don't know.

Let's look for more clues.

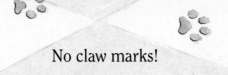

No claw marks!

Now look at the other tracks—the tracks that go to the dog's dish.

Did you ever watch a cat walk?

A cat walks on four feet. But the tracks of his hind feet fall exactly on the tracks of his front feet. So his footprints are one behind the other, in one line. They look like the footprints of an animal with only two feet. A cat pulls his claws in when he walks. So he does not leave claw marks.

11

Now do you know who drank the milk? (THE DOG!)

Now do you know who ate the dog food? (THE CAT!)

The footprints of a fox are in a single line, like a cat's footprints. But they have claw marks, like a dog's.

What kind of footprints does a rabbit make? You can see that a rabbit has little front paws and big hind feet.

The little front paws will make little paw prints. The big hind feet will make big tracks.

13

Now, here is another problem for a nature detective:
Who went lickety-split across the snow?
A rabbit, of course. But which way did he go?
Did he go to the tree? Or did he go away from the tree?
It looks as if he went toward the tree, doesn't it?

You can see the marks of the front paws ahead of the big hind feet.

But do you know how a rabbit jumps? Look at that!

When a rabbit jumps, he puts his big hind feet ahead of his front paws.

What happened here on a snowy day?

You can see the rabbit tracks in the snow.

You know which way they are going.

All at once the rabbit tracks are far apart.

This means the rabbit began to take big jumps.

He was in a hurry. Why?

Did you see those tracks coming out of the woods?

Those footprints have claw marks like a dog's.

But they are in a *single* line, like the tracks of a cat.

Who could have made those tracks? There is only one answer. . . .

A fox!

Now you know why the rabbit was in a hurry!

Did the fox catch the rabbit? Look again at the picture on page 17.

Look carefully.

There are big hoofprints in the mud near the river.
And there are little hoofprints, too.
Who was here?

19

It was a mother deer and her baby fawn. They came to the river for a drink.

Somebody sat down on the
muddy bank of the river. Who?

This is the mark of a round, fat belly.

These back footprints were made by webbed feet.

And somebody made the track that goes right into the water.

21

A bullfrog came out of the river. He sat on the muddy bank to rest.

And only a snake leaves a track like that. A snake came down to the river. Then he slithered into the water.

Here are more tracks in the mud near the river.
And there is a little pile of empty shells, too.
They are crayfish shells.

The tracks look something like the hands and feet of a baby. But look at those long claws!

A raccoon made those tracks. Raccoons like to catch crayfish and eat them. So now you know what happened. A raccoon had dinner here last night. He found crayfish in the river. He ate the crayfish. And he left the shells in a little pile.

A nature detective can find many clues on a sandy beach.
When you walk on the beach in the morning,
look for sea gull tracks. They can tell you which way
the wind was blowing when the gulls were there.

Like airplanes, sea gulls take off facing into the wind.
First the gulls must run along the sand to get up speed
for takeoff. As they run, their toes dig deeper into the sand.
Here all the gull toe tracks are in a line facing east.
So you know that the wind came from the east.

Tracks are good clues for a nature detective.
But there are other clues, too.

Who lives here?

Who ate here?

A nature detective learns to look and listen—and smell.
She can find clues in a backyard, in the woods, or in a city park.

Who made that smell?

Do you know who made these tracks?

30

Follow the tracks and see.

31

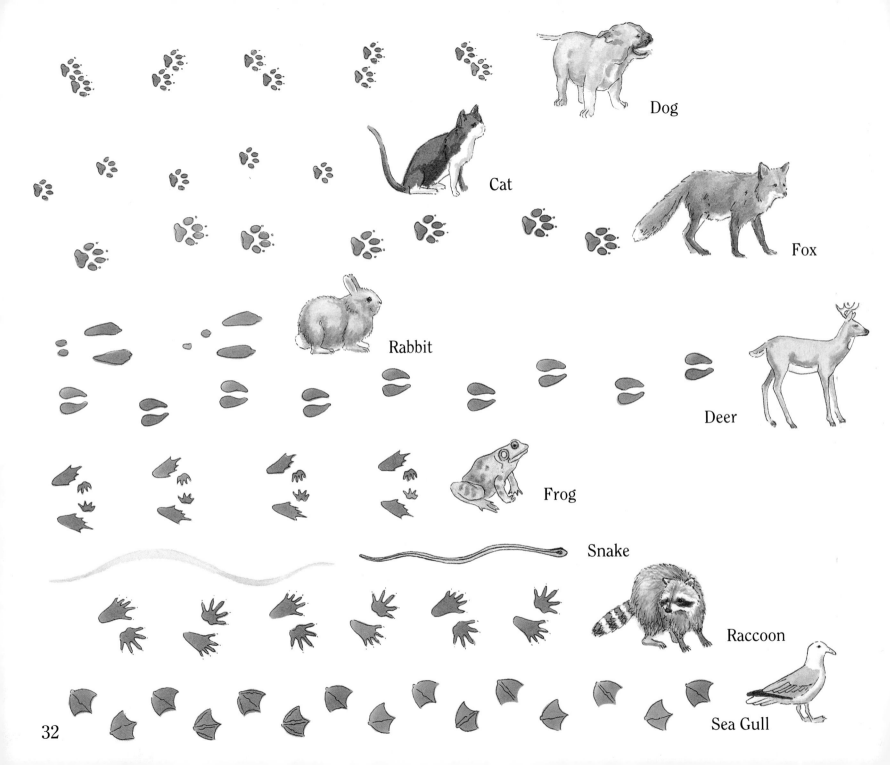

Dog

Cat

Fox

Rabbit

Deer

Frog

Snake

Raccoon

Sea Gull

32